Annabella of Ely

ANNABELLA OF ELY

POEMS: I-LXXVII

Foreword by

Liesl Ketum

gnOme

gnOme books
gnomebooks.wordpress.com

Please address inquiries to:
gnomebooks@gmail.com

Cover image: Alexandrina Maria da Costa, public
domain,
http://www.mysticsofthechurch.com/2009/11/blesse
d-alexandrina-da-costa-mystic-and.html

ISBN-13: 978-0692709573 (Custom)
ISBN-10: 0692709576

St. Rita of Cascia, patron Saint of the Impossible,
sickness, and wounds.

Foreword

Upon arriving at the carved baroque doors of the University of Belgrade's Rare Book Library, I could never have imagined to discover the misplaced musings of the young woman who some once called "the little one in One," Annabella of Ely (1884-1917). It is said that the beautiful young miracle worker who, in her twenty-ninth year fell chronically ill, chose to live a simple life of poverty. Juggling periodic states of health with intense sickness, her body never quite recovered, though her heart, in solitude, grew continuously closer to God. One day she became so stricken that passersby, alarmed by her declining state, went to the nearest convent and implored the nuns to aid her. The abbess, knowing full well of Annabella's strict holy life in God, ordered her nuns to fetch Annabella (against her will) from her makeshift cot. The nuns brought her back to live with them, but she was never entirely brought back to life. Often being too sick to move from bed, Annabella lived out her remaining days, totaling just less than four years, in the abbey. She was cared for by three devout Catholic nuns whom she liked to call her "ambulans angeli" (walking angels).

Little known in her day, yet known in Ely for her sharp wit and thoughtful charm, Annabella was frequently visited by pious locals who wished to secure her blessing. Folklore discloses that she soon took to writing poetry in order to honor and document her alternating pangs of disease and spiritual ascent. She is said to have written all of her work on a single roll of parchment measuring eleven inches wide by seven feet long. Although she suffered many physical maladies, her dystonia in particular presented a unique challenge while writing. The nuns found that, rather than fumbling about with loose leaves of paper, a single roll of parchment aided her writing practice. Her work, replete with strange, bewildering brevity, yet managing to house a distinctive spiritual philosophy, was long thought to be inadvertently thrown on her funeral pyre. A modern pyre was indeed an odd request in the winter of 1917, but it was what she had specifically noted in her will, and the Abbess acquiesced. The ceremony was held on Eventide Priory's 26-acre property at a remote clearing where the forest opened to the sea.

Needless to say, I was astonished to find a large portion (it had been neatly cut in half!) of her misplaced poems hidden within another old manuscript, *The Sutras of Banko Agni*, when the book fell to the floor. How did such a large roll of parchment fit inside another book, you might ask? Well, *The Sutras* had been hollowed out and the *Seventy-Seven Poems* had been folded—and refolded, many times—in order to fit inside. Where are Banko Agni's sutras? I have no idea. And as to why *half* of Annabella's work was hidden inside that old hollowed out book? It is surely a mystery to me. But it is by this accidental act of bibliomancy that these blackened Love poems have come to meet me. And it is my hope that you will welcome them into your life just as I have.

I've done my best to present the poems by the order in which they were written. The manuscript itself seemed wont in hiding things. Though Annabella initially ordered her poems numerically, something strange happens as one moves one's eyes down the unrolled parchment. In some cases, poems are written upside-down. In other cases poems are literally written over top of one another, almost scrambling themselves into amorphous, nonsensical anti-poems. I cannot say what Annabella's reasons were for doing this; I cannot say, that is, simply because I do not know. It could be completely ambiguous, the work of tired, pain-writhed hands. Or it could be the remnants of an eccentric writing habit of hers, perhaps another mode by which she self-naughted. On that matter, you, dear reader, are free to form your own opinion.

Even more curious, despite barely being able to hold a writing utensil without the greatest discomfort, her penmanship was exquisite, so neatly and beautifully done that, had one not known she had no training in it, her written words might pass as blackletter calligraphy. But what lies hidden underneath such artful beauty was some-*thing* more beautiful still: the exquisite corpse of her writing self, a holy spectre figure that wished to be neither Annabella nor anyone else. Herein beauty is marked by a weird insistence on leaving herself behind, a dead woman kneeling angelically on the tattered steps of the divine.

The following text is short, but one thing is for certain. There is something quite peculiar about her verse, as it performs a kind of experimental poeticism that just does not quite fit previous molds. And so, we might do best simply to call her a heretic amongst heretics.

Liesl Ketum,
Humbert Divinity School
April 21, 2016

I

Death is the frail king. Death, the ornery dirge of naught! But naught can death be, and so this I see, that death is weakling and kindling for its own bones.

II

This is the comet of Death, and my body weeps in infected drips, and rains its own boiling stew. This is it; this is innards' drip. I am the non-place where "me" must de facto die and All will breathe.

III

The body, inconclusive... and yet, soreness and in pain. And fistulae tunnel in the unending funnel of a life lived within me. But when I am not, and "me" does not want, then All reigns— and the body bloats in the singing moat of disappearance.

IV

I, in the mystery of unfolding gloom, harness
strength in strength's demise, know weakness
through strength, and find subtlety in my un-
knowing this: that the body houses nothing.
There is nothing but wind in the body. And my
bones are stellar blood moats.

V

You are I personified, and we barely can. And
none is *I* intensified, but nothing all the same.
And me is all minus All, derived of mottled
grout. And All knows the nevermore of knowing
nothing still.

VI

And so I spring forth, spiraling like a phantom in
a hall of moths, to be myself always and never
again. And so I am all winded up and unwinding
always still, unstill and always winding,
pouncing onto the moon to sit on a twirling
silver rock.

VII

To imagine that, in a pit of fermenting moon
rays, stands thankfulness staring into the me I
once was. And to see—knowing that my eyes are
blinded by their own sight. These are two
modalities with which the moonlight hurls Joy
into the world.

VIII

In my dreams and in my dances, as the wintered
whores walk by, there is no one here but a
whirling wind... a gleaming insistence, by the by.
Through these woods and on these shores, I hear
You sing so sweetly. I cannot not know Your
voice and not sit gently weeping.

IX

Eyes of blueish and wavering, talking to me
bluely with the night-like hollow of Your
whispering breath. Lips speak of inverted mores,
puckering. We sit in this holy grove, leaving
alone the crooked branches, so that the trees
may take their shapes.

X

And I will speak of nothing and know nothing.
And we will roll about the hay like young lovers.
Dispensing with the sun's rays and whirring in
the wind. Appealing to the moon and laughing
with the darkness.

XI

Apples from a tree of light fall in hidden
trajectories which shoot out of their being and
into the darkness. Squashed and juiced am I; a
pie for a maelstrom, sauced and perplexed.

XII

Three tattered steps I take across this floor of
nails. And against my better judgment, my feet
throw up in wails. But just then I realize, and
have known it all along, that it is You who built
this floor and so I'll sing a song.

XIII

To look upon a photograph of oneself and simply
say, "I am." And to know that in that place
stands no one at all. A picture is worth a
thousand remembrances that there need be no
person there. And so I kiss my photograph a
thousand times for its teachings.

XIV

Sadness is the place of woe and this weight drips
tears from dandered eyes. But your weight-rain
drops as eye drops and this "me" drops out of I.
Just as the floor drops out when I drop You in,
so sadness gives way to the Joy that this battered
body brings.

XX

There is an astral balloon that holds me in so
tightly, squeezing the flowing juices of being
from my body. My tongue cannot taste a thing
and I am whirling like a whittling wooden
dancer made of sand.

XXI

A tongue which cannot lick sits inside a cage of
stammering brainwaves, absorbing everything
other than my love for God. I cannot taste a
thing and all tastes so sweet: my mind is like a
fever buttered in honey.

XXII

My stomach is a harness which holds three
square meals on top a balance beam of opposite
poles. On the one side sits the saints of all time.
On the other side sits all devils. Lightly tonguing
the bang-clanking of soiled dishes, these taste
buds foretell the End of Time.

XXIII

Four distant stars and our Sun throw pellets of
brain-melting bliss at the world. All I can do is
intensely watch closely, for behind the veil of the
banes of the world is the harvest center of all
cosmic Joy.

XXIV

I speak in numbers and count in words, and in
due time I lost the way. But beneath the rocks of
the crumby path to nowhere sits an oven
forever-baking seven loaves of manna. I cannot
taste them, but I know they are wonderfully
sweet!

XXV

I'm sure I am not the first woman driven mad by
Your beauty. I cannot even tell anyone anything
about You, because when I speak with them, I
am muted by Your incidence. Even a mundane
conversation with the most impish of scoundrels
holds a clinic on the nature of bliss.

XXVI

A plentiful heart beats with the meandering
drone of a swaying crooked tree. Croaks and
creeks bemoan the meek! These exclamations
are the eczema of our kingly kind of moaning,
one which searches by seizing.

XXVII

There is a glorious wench at the edge of hell.
Like a womb-worm, she bears the hidden name
of the crypto-elemental; waxing etymological,
she is the scorching Duchess of the auto-
empyreal.

XXVIII

It is I who am this pyre, a mortal coiled in hell's
fire. Then again, who dies in death? ... so this
"me" in my I perspires. All this, All sets ablaze.
Flaming and wafting; smoke within smoke
beyond smoke.

XXIX

Upon this flame, I dance alone. Heaven sent,
this hell dethrones. This me I once thought that I
am, is now not: not nor/nor neither.

XXX

It is so hot here. And I am burning. If you cover your ears, I will tell you how and why I burn, and uncover them for you. And then we will burn together.

XXXI

Do not listen to a single word I say. And do not not listen either. Just burn with me, if you wish, in this mystical fire. And if you do not yet wish to do so, then do not fear. I will never stop burning.

XXXII

A mind so dead it dangles gently, over the mountain's top. There thine own heart finally beats... fervor abreast of infinity and then... a pop!

XXXIII

Candles blown out in these petering gusts of
wind, just as a baited mealworm knows, but
cannot know, how its body must eventually
rescind.

XXXIV

Underneath a pit of duress, I reach my hand
through into a life unlived. I shiver in fear and
light another candle. I shiver no more, yet
always shiver, and I breathe again.

XXXV

Seventy-seven trillion manifestations appear
each time I open my eyes. I am blinded with
eternity's breath as I suck on dry grains of rice.
Mucosal and multi-layered, You pull me over the
wet edge of time.

XXXVI

Wretched a wench am I when I try to clean a space for You. For, You dirty me completely with suffering, and so I roll around like a pig in the mud.

XXXVII

I call to my spirit that I have not suffered enough. And just then a bird is eaten by its own egg and a serpent in white genuflects against the crowded room.

XXXVIII

I am the lowest level of scum. Beyond my tears sits my being beyond tears. Yet, without these tears of death, immanent joy exists not.

XXXIX

This ecstasy lasts forever, but my ambulans
angeli tell me it lasts for only minutes at a time. I
am so blood-sick that lightning shoots from my
shriveling veins: the unclotting of eternity.

XL

Scorned, I am vileness. I am so gruesome.
Collapsed, I am hideousness. Prolapsed and
sighing, I wave a finger into the air and inhale
the diseased stench of myself.

XLI

My skin is wilting as I melt on this cross with
You. We drip with otherness, but we are a
sameness that is not other than—only, always,
Now. This abyss, Your cross; my womb, an abyss
for Melquiadian splendors.

XLII

You can have my blood if you need it. Here is my heart—only for You— beating with the crimson tides of elongated rays of fire. Will my living heart revive the lost reveries of these thousand thousand deaths? Is death my own heart beating as You?

XLIII

The ocean liner of my heart sinks into a sea of pain. These tear ducts drip, falling as the world, a veil of tears made of gray rain. In this rain-world of treading sea-pain, I hope for nothing but to kiss You again.

XLIV

Like a wizard's queen, I drape these soft sheets over my wormhole eyes. A sinking ship made of lead, my bare body indents the bed. (You indent my soul.) Capsized by captivation, unmoving as a block of white ice, I subsist only by Your thrice.

XLV

Feline is the sea witch who would hold me away
from You. Yet this ocean parts, as her cauldron
starts, to boil a way through. I tread my legs with
all I have, drowning in Your seas. And as I die, I
see without eyes, that Your oceans part for me.

XLVI

My third eye looks out the snout of a pig, so dirty
and so wise. In the mud, we roll about, our hair
encroached by lice. It is by these paths of grime
that we come to know true pain, and by
unending pain alone will pain finally end.

XLVII

I am eviscerated by Your incidence, the absence
which retreats as presence. Where art Thou?
(Certainly not here.) In between shivering
bewilderment and bewildered shivering, I am
expunged by the ghostly matrimony of
androgyny.

XLVIII

A cross upon my heart and I hope to die before I
die. Bring me nothing but a cup of water, for I
see behind the veil an ocean of splendor.
Swimming in the moonlight, we walk together
on water. A halo is placed o'er the head of the
floating Androgyne.

XLIX

There's a strange dreamer staring at me through
the wood. She sees that I love You. She knows
the things I cannot know. I am petrified; become
of the wall which holds me away from You. I am
terrified; but through this wall I will walk into
You.

L

I pay the price for this life with my life. I am a
butterfly. I am stomach acid. Feeling sick and
befuddled, I vomit-cry energetic, dancing tears
out of spinning spider eyes.

LI

Flabbergasted, I am aghast. Aghast, I,
flabbergasted, am. Four foul flubs am I in this
garner-chamber, awaiting absolutely nothing.

LII

This is my cross to bear. It is no different than if
it were not. (Nothing is more important than
anything else.) Pity me not, for this pain is no
different than a laughing goat in a field of gray
corn stalks; a goose in a mire; a platypus giggling
on a cloud of hay.

LIII

I have felt loneliness. I have felt kindness. I have
felt otherness, awaiting me beyond these walls I
keep. I have been mummified. I have been
calcified. I have been terrified behind the walls I
keep.

LIV

I cannot believe myself. I cannot bereave myself.
I cannot beget myself, among the whores of
sleep. Tell me something all too true. Tell me
something I can't spew. Tell me something to
release me from the harangued pangs of sleep.

LV

Mighty in the sloppy mud. Sloppy is the mighty
drudge. Callous is the soul unkempt in the halls
of sleep. Trying not to walk this way. Dying to
die another day. Living to lie another night in
the bed of sleep.

LVI

Crepuscule of lonesome hour—in this sleep, All
is devoured. I cannot retain anything in the
casket of Sleep. Of this no-thing, stolen fire. On
these coals, stills the mire. I am sleeping and I
still weep.

LVII

A whistling gypsy knocked on the door of my
sleep. An infidel throws stones at the feet of my
sleep. A beautiful whore kisses the death of my
sleep. A serpent is at my sleep. All this sleep.
Sleep.

LVIII

Sleep. Sleep is anyone. Sleep is no good for no
one. Sleep is everyone not staying awake. Sleep
is tired eyes of the face of Everyman. Sleep is
never the not I need to wake me up from sleep.

LIX

For the love of God, wake me up from this Sleep.
I am everything so that you may wake up. For
the love of God, wake me up from this Sleep.
Follow nothing into awake.

LX

I cannot see that I believe out of my eyes.
Believed, cannot eyes see out of I. Eyes believe
not that I cannot see. To see is to believe that I
believe I cannot be.

LXI

Being not and being alive, I warp the river's
edge. In this storm, a fish is born to feed
Ariadne's thread: the thread that knots the
barren lands together to my life, a life that is but
is not is, and so, yields the opposite of strife.

LXII

Crawling in the nightmare of this me-without-
You, I fall asleep again. Sleeping in terror are the
terrors of sleep. In this double sleep dream, I
stare into my eyelids, the apt pupil of my auto-
dilating pupils. My amygdala, taut and gyrating,
points the bone of death at sleep's covered eyes.
I open to the awakening of bliss.

LXIII

Lights glow aflutter in the corner and I smile for
You. I am the *this* which points the Way and You
point back to me as *I*. I spin hurlingly into more
jetting smiles, look up to the ceiling, and know
the doorway has been opened. I cannot not
smile.

LXIV

I smile a grin so large, long and splayed out as if
on the rack of Being. An angel hovers over my
head, but I cannot see him. He bobs inside-out
and upside-down as I lay down in order to meet
him.

LXV

We meet as a Smile. We are smiles eating our
tears. We are glowing hues of yellow, light-
scapes of red and orange; eternal fiery
glowworms bound by divine treaty.

LXVI

Wrapped in a blanket of fire, I inhale the soft,
cold death of the earth. And there are things
which words can do that require nothing at all
but dearth. Viscous yet chiming, my diction
rings only of God.

LXVII

Whirled and corpse-sick, this corpus eats its own
words. Absently plentiful, amassing tigers for
grave worms, I sit on a cradle made of golden
stone. To melt is to make it neither happen nor
happen not, pure like purring happenstance.

LXVIII

Comets stream out of my body—a Tabriz rug of
cosmic Love threaded by my malady. Burning
bones and brush reveal the route of the unpaved
road meandered. On this road, in a nimble room
reserved for Grace, is a zone amid bliss and
paralytic spittle.

LXIX

My style, corrosive and full of blood; hollowed
out oxen rolling in mud. Hounded, I wail at the
moon; and sculpted, waxing and waning,
prostrating before the eclipse.

LXX

I close my eyes and see an x-ray of my skeleton.
Within this skin is nothing but wind, the absence
that fills so that I can truly live. Walk with me,
thine angels, and then blow me over the cusp of
this pink mountain.

LXXI

"Never! Never!" Wounded at the heart-center of
the nine rivers, my spirit impales the sea. My
mind, the cleft lip of derangement, tramples over
pink hay—wandering unfollowed into the union
station of Heaven.

LXXII

Life. Life is here. Life is what we need and what
we see. Death. Death is near. Death is the full
hole that makes life be. Digging the grave of my
life, I wade through this hole with the dead.

LXXIII

I was never married. (I long only for God.) I
point to a crowd of nuns and they give a gnomic
nod. It's the absent nod of ever-presence, under
the cover of an unwed heart, the heart that beats
without You, even when you've left me naught.
Heart-coitus made on a weeping throne.

LXXIV

Long shall We know this river's flow. It flows
nowhere and Our spout is tapped with rain
water. The spout pours out nothing. In that
mode, we reign. And this river's ocean floats a
buoy made of sand, as a blinking, milky siren
holds out her gracious hand.

LXXV

Ever bouncing, like eggs hatching nothings,
volcanic splendors, I slip inside the earth to
touch His face. He sneaks out, always, and goes
nowhere; remaining, un-seeable, right Here: this
heaving predicament of existence is the
unknowable face of God.

LXXVI

Exploding everywhere—in this crisp, wanton
air—the eyes of God are of no compare! For, to
compare the world with the Lord Almighty is to
touch the Son with the sun's own light streams.
Here we stand and we always fall, for in this pit
All jumps through walls. I am the wall that lets
You in. And, dear reader, you are Our kin.

LXXVII

Autotelic Joy surrounds our fears and
unendingly consumes us ...

*(Text ends. Parchment is neatly
ripped at this point.—LK)*

gnOme is a secret press specializing in the publication of anonymous, pseudepigraphical, and apocryphal works from the past, present, and future.

"The child received at the Font the name of Lydwine . . . derived from the Flemish word 'lyden,' to suffer" (Huysmans).

gnOme is acephalic. Book sales support the authors.

GNOMEBOOKS.WORDPRESS.COM

Other titles from gnOme

A & N • *Autophagiography*

Brian O'Blivion • *Blackest Ever Hole*

Cergat • *Earthmare: The Lost Book of Wars*

Eva Clanculator • *Atheologica Germanica*

Ars Cogitanda • *footnote to* silence

M • *Un-Sight/ Un-Sound (delirium X.)*

M.O.N. • *ObliviOnanisM*

Pseudo-Leopardi • *Cantos for the Crestfallen*

I. P. Snooks *Be Still, My Throbbing Tattoo*

Rasu-Yong Tugen, Baroness De Tristeombre •
Songs from the Black Moon

Subject A • *Verses from the Underlands*

Y.O.U. • *How to Stay in Hell*

HWORDE

Nab Saheb and Denys X. Arbaris • *Bergmetal:
Oro-Emblems of the Musical Beyond*

N • *Hemisphere Eleven*

Yuu Seki • *Serial Kitsch*

www.ingramcontent.com/pod-product-compliance
Lightning Source LLC
Chambersburg PA
CBHW021148020426
42331CB00005B/958